Enchanter
of the **Soul**

Enchanter
of the **Soul**

Poems by
Sreevas Sreedhar

Published by

**GULF BOOK
SERVICES**

To My Beloved

Pavitra, Pranav & Rashmi

❧

"When you find someone with the same
mental illness as you....
Priceless!"

———

Amrita Pritam
Indian Novelist & Poet

❧

"I'm made of words and rivers
& winds and wild flowers.
I'm part grief and part hope
& all love."

———

Victoria Erickson
Rhythms and Roads

GULF BOOK SERVICES

Published by Gulf Book Services Ltd
20-22 Wenlock Road, London,
NI 7GU,UK

Email: info@gulfbooks.co.uk

Illustrations by Rashmi Kulkarni (Sprout Design)

First Published International Edition in 2024

ISBN: 978-1-917529-01-3
Year: October 2024

About the Author

Sreevas Sreedhar

Sreevas Sreedhar is originally from the Indian state of Kerala. He moved to UAE in 1999. Since then, he is living in the Emirate of Dubai.

In the process of compiling this book, he has translated several of his own poems from Malayalam* to English. His initial foray into poetry is chronicled in the work titled "Enchanter of the Soul".

"ENCHANTER OF THE SOUL"
is his debut collection of poetry.

*The official language of Kerala, a southern state in India.

Contents

To My Beloved

My beloved,
Forbear not such sorrowful cries.
I'm bound to echo your refrain,
Unable to withhold my own.

Your hair smells of marigold,
When they are charmingly braided.

My beloved,
Forever I'm obsessed with your eyes,
whilst they are inked.
Your gaze illuminates and mystifies my soul.

My beloved,
Your loving hymns kissed my
heart with a healing grace.

My soul is destined for despair, forever unsettled.
Till I breathe my last breath for thee,
For thee alone, I'd tread paths faithlessly.

Let me not get shattered!
My destiny is to sip the wine divine and plunge,
Into the abyss of fervent dreams, let it be mine.

Until the whispering winds reveal,
That you could never love
A flawed adorer like me.
I beg for your forgiveness!

Fluent Silence

In the depths of night,
my dreams unfurl,
profound they swirl.

Your beauty stirs my soul,
Fragile yet distilled,
As passions roll.

In the luminous glow of
love's tender thread,
the flowers blossomed on my
solitary shore.

Ever shall I endeavor
seeking your honest smile.
In love's vibrant hues
That feels like heavenly bliss.

Don't love me for reasons.
Don't leave me in despair.
I wish not to lose the serenity,
Of a mind attuned into love.

The moon wanes,
The dreams dissipate.
Prelude to my own,
Flowing silence.

With Love

In shadows deep,
I lingered long.
As the nights regal bloom unfurled
In solitude I faced the world.

My thoughts, adrift, sought solace
Yet tomorrow's essence did deceit.

Tears, like pearls, fell from my eyes
Breeding deceits, truth in disguise.

For greed's allure, we're torn apart
In heart and flesh, a shattered art.

Alone we stand, in silent plea
Only for love.

Being Lonely

Soft hues of yellow,
Dancing through the pane.
He clung to the lattice, verdant and
serene.

Bougainvillea's unfurl,
As he yearns for his love,
Amid whispers of a bygone spring.

In sunlight's embrace,
A moth in muted gray
Swirls with squirrels, restless.

The clouds sailed as soft cotton,
adorning the sailor's dawn hue.
Night dissolves into the sea's canvas,
clouds shimmering like powdered sugar.

In twilight's embrace, fireflies dance,
Breathing light into the essence of existence.

Amid their radiant flight,
Discordant whispers emerge from crickets' song.

The flicker of lights, a fleeting waltz,
Ephemeral glimmers fade into the night.

Shadows stir, a silent symphony,
Instilling whispers of fear in the soul's depths.

Under the weight of darkness' cloak,
Eyes heavy with dreams, surrender.
In the quiet expanse, where shadows reign,
A dance of light and dark unfolds.

Euphoric Minds

Upon rain's descent
Serenity hovers.

Moist clouds caress to,
Stroke a canvas in the misty sky.

Subtle scent of earth,
Gentle whispers of soil,
Each fluorescent droplets,
Ignite memories that
Radiates minds Euphoria.

Curly Blue

In the realm of my existence
'Curly Blue' did dwell where
dreams, in eternal lament,
Forever knelled.

Within her tearful gaze
Water lilies unfurled in a constant swell.

Her eyes spoke to me in silence.
Beseeching my hopeful spirit to embrace
The love of a lifetime's tender grace.

Let me confess
That my love has kissed her soul.

Her lack of comprehension
makes me fragile and feeble.

The love dwindles,
I regret for being
here and staying
alive only for her.

Yet, one day
I shall journey back,
To where my heart truly
belongs.

Loves Burial

Crimson blooms, love's embrace they weave,
Tulips affection, they believe
Angels' serenade to hearts they impart,
Entwine in love's ocean, to surrender and depart.

In this realm of love,
where essence fades away,
Breathless, they succumb,
in passions sway.

Yet they discern, in the
depths they delve, Love, a
bestowal of fondness, it shall
forever dwell.

Eternal eludes, infinite it's
not, Love, a gift of
tenderness, in every plot.

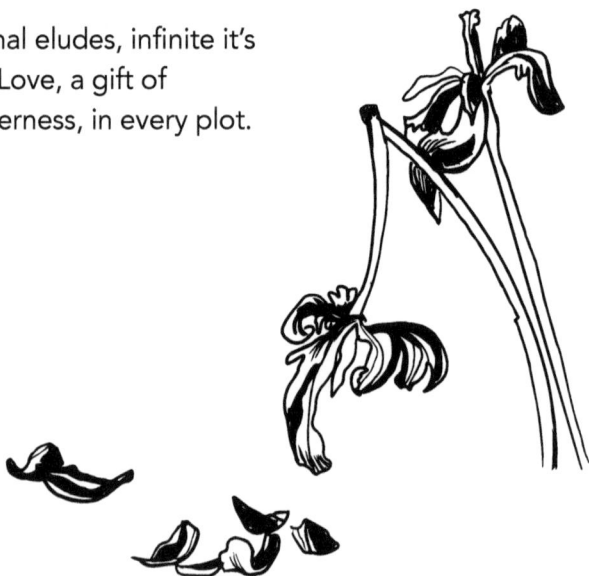

A Celestial Maestro

I savored another sip
of divine drink.

I gently realize
My blissful soul awakens gently into
the essence of a celestial musician.

Unglued from my realm,
A self-inflicted curse
I transform into a butterfly unmarred.

From within, a heart bleeds, yet overflows with grace,
Descending to this earth, seeking love's elusive trace.

In quest of that tender bloom, fragile and rare,
I dance amid the meadows, lost in nature's flair.

In the gentle glow of my soul's voyage,
I seek not to allure, but to grace,
With a love deep-rooted, enduring,
A passion unbidden, yet embraced.

Ready to yield, I stand,
Before the altar of your ardent affection,
Forever yours, in this timeless dance.

Blue Rose

May I wander through the
corridors of memory?
Where moments, like raindrops,
cascade gracefully.
Transporting me to the euphoria of discovery,
In the arms of love.

In dreams, the passion burns, a crimson fire,
Hues of yellow and roses dipped in sapphire.
In quiet gazes and tender smiles, desire,
Wrapped in the embrace of hope
And the fullness of love.

In whispers of longing, in silence keen,
I trace the echoes of footsteps unseen,
Yearning to know where you've been!

The Love Spy

In the dance of shadows, life's embrace,
Where certainty dissolves in haze,
A soul liberated seeks its grace,
Amidst the labyrinth, love's gentle craze.

In pursuit, amidst the twilight's gleam,
Where doubts and passions intertwine,
In the realm where dreams and doubts convene,
I sought the elusive, the divine.

Whether distant or close,
In the celestial expanse or
Upon this soil.

Until our paths converge once more,
I yearn fervently,
to be the concealed embodiment
of her affection.

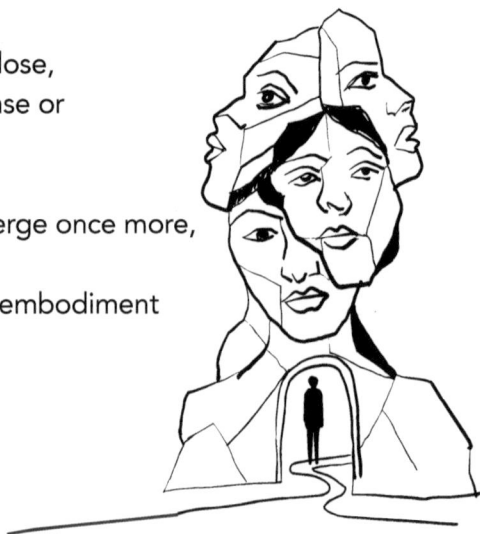

Being Soulless

Never did I imagine
Your disdain could pierce me so.

What deed of mine hath
brought this rue?

Do not shy away,
Nor veil your sight
To feign my absence.

As the moon dims,
And stars fracture
in the heavens,
The night descends
with bitter chill.

Let not this truth
be our fate,
For I feel my heart ablaze,
fading into the ether.
My spirit, once crystal,
And dreams once vivid,
now lies shattered.

Enfold me in your
embrace once more!
I shall descend, enthralling,
Into the depths,
And in the gentle
arms of oblivion,
Unbound, we sway.

To A Childhood Friend

On a glorious spring dawn,
Bathed in the golden light's adorn,
She graced my world, a vision to see,
With eyes of emerald, enchanting my gaze.

Not all beheld her eyes' allure,
Save for me, love's only cure.
In her curls danced the gentle air,
And I melted in her soul's affair.

Every look she gave sparked flames,
A love's embrace, a heartfelt desire.
In dreams, we roamed the verdant fields,
Where misty veils the apple yields.

In lush woods, our footsteps tread,
Beside green ponds, we shared our bed.
Her fingers intertwined with mine,
Her head upon my shoulder, divine.

I close my eyes, feel the tender touch,
Of her lashes damp with love's clutch.
With passion's fervor, I still recall,
The mysteries hidden within her gaze's thrall.

Poets Agony

In a room softly lit,
By bedside lamps that gently lit,
Metaphors dance, memories rise
With wine-soaked cigar,
my muse defies.

Within this dim-lit space,
I feel the well of ideas embrace,
Drained dry, a whispered sigh,
As creativity seems to shy.

Beneath relentless rain,
I wander in dreams of distant grace.
Rainbows dance in radiant hue,
Their charm, a lovely plumage.

Restless, my soul in endless roam,
Through vacant spaces, it seeks thy home.
Yearning for warmth in this chill,
To find solace in thy love's gentle thrill.

Rhythms of the Rain

In the embrace of rains soft kiss,
Trees adorned with jeweled drops,
Leaves shimmer, barks glisten,
Nature's love, in verdant hush.

A beetle dances upon the bark's stage,
Lost in the labyrinth of moist foliage,
A weaver ant, in silken sanctuary,
Crafts its world, snug and airy.

Nearby, a bird trembles on a bough,
Its feathers adorned with grace,
In the symphony of rain's embrace,
Each creature finds its sacred place.

I endure within this realm,
Merely to dance with her.
In the rapture of melding with rain
before it wanes,
Leaving behind its enchanting scent.

With eyes shut tight, I conjure,
Her lovely visage, dissolving
into mist!

She's Alive

On a scorching day, unexpected,
Rain descended softly, its mournful call.

Beneath its gentle touch, flowers wilted,
Beneath a light mist, their colors sprawl.

In whispers heard amidst the moistened air,
The wind did rise, a tempest's tender song.

I shut the window, seeking warmth to spare,
Before my coffee's comfort had been gone.

Upon the couch, I nestled, cozy-bound,
Listening to rain's sweet serenade.

Its melody a dance, cascading down,
As sunlight pierced through the storm's veil.

I gazed aloft, where clouds obscure the blue,
And there she blossomed, like an Angel's grace.

Adorned with rain, a radiant debut,
Her fleeting presence in that somber space.

Enraptured by her beauty, she swiftly departed,
And with her, the rain came to an eternal halt.

In that enchanting moment, I witnessed,
A glimpse of heaven, in her earthly bound.

Lost in the Rain

As raindrops dance,
in ecstasy I soar.

Within the cadence of the downpour's roar,
I spin and sway, in nature's sweet refrain,
Sighing deeply, in this celestial domain.

In rain's embrace, my spirit finds its flight,
A blissful union in the veiled night's light.

A Bleeding Soul

Allow me to savor wine,
And dream about you.

The pleasure of dreaming you,
flourishes this lustrous night.

My beloved,
My soul is infused in alcohol.
Allow me to savor wine,
And dream about you.

I'm blissfully obsessed
And spoiled in your beauty, Imbued in my heart.
My beloved, I live for a reason.

My soul is immersed in the
Enchantment of your love.
Allow me to savor wine,
And dream about you.

In this world of wretched happiness,
Your loving memories shine in the dark.

Rekindling my spirit
With a heart that aches.
The warmth of your love
That has nestled within my heart.

I wish I could blossom again,
Into a celestial flower.

Radiating a loving fragrance
within the confines of your
Perfumed garden.

Blonde Night

In a night veiled with the essence of prose,
The chill wind whispered its ancient tale.
Towards the café's embrace, our steps did flow,
Where 'Leffe Blonde' awaited in the ale.

A dream girl with a pearl's luminescent glow,
And with words profound and grave;
'Eat here, or we both starve'.

Sea's treasures in a bowl,
Calamari fries, thickly cut with care,
Glistening with mayonnaise's tender kiss,
Immersed in the moment, beyond compare,
Like a sponge, the spirit did blissfully immerse.

That night, silence draped the Western skies,
I'm not alone, the Road we both pursue.
Beside me, a companion, no disguise,
Walking alongside, amidst unfamiliar shores.

Nightmare

On a windy night
In the chilly air
Under the cover of darkness
The creatures of the night
In the company of the prince of shadows,
Ventured forth into a crafted antiquity.

    Wheels etched upon the dampened trail,
    A throng of felines in pursuit,
    Some clad in ashen hues,
    Their amber eyes alight,
    With a creepy stare,
    Growls and hisses echoing.

Baring their gleaming teeth,
Sharp as the keenest blade,
Heartbeats quicken,
Sending shivers down the spine.

    In the early hours of dawn,
    As darkness still reigns,
    Longing for the touch of the sun's first light,
    Yearning to quench the ceaseless torment.

I awaken,
To the sound of a tender hiss,
My solitary gray-furred cat
Casting upon me with her unsettling gaze.

Perfumed Soul

Into my life you gracefully tread,
Infusing my soul.
With your scent, a fragrance from divine realms,
I yearn to worship,
Endlessly entwined.

I ardently desire
to adore your alluring
scent and longing to be
eternally yours.

But I realize
You find joy in paths aloof.
Though my heart aches in silent plea,
I release you,
Knowing you're meant to be free.

Memories Never Fade

Much to my dismay,
I found it quite startling
That my recent letter eluded your grasp.

I bid adieu to the memories,
Only to find myself lonely and secluded.

The repercussions of solitary being,
They tangle every thread that life's weave.

In the void of memories, I find solace,
Gazing into your beautiful gaze,
Stirring the depths of longing,
Seeking the very essence of love's grace.
Silent echoes weave their intricate dance,
In the symphony of stillness, wild and grand.

In the garden of your eyes, flowers gracefully unfurl,
I'm enchanted within your mysteries.

Starless Night

The starless night
Enfolds me within its
embrace.

My shadow harbors the
plethora of profound
darkness.

Shadows swirl and twirl
chanting the unadorned
mantra.

Stumbled in the darkness
crumbled into a vortex
embracing the eclipse.
Tears welling and
cascading down my
cheeks.
Smeared the rouge
I comprehend that,
the life is same as it
is enduring through
the ages!

Before I turn into dust

Let me imbibe the essence of wine,
And let my thoughts be consumed by you.

Tonight, under the shimmering stars,
Your presence blooms like a rare flower.

Oh, my cherished one,
My spirit intertwines with the spirits in the wine.
Let me sip from the cup of dreams,
And let my fantasies dance with your silhouette.

In the depths of my soul,
Your beauty resides as a cherished treasure.
I am intoxicated by your allure,
Lost in the ecstasy of your love.

Grant me this moment to relish the wine,
While visions of you enchant my mind.

In this world of fleeting joys,
Your memory casts a radiant glow in the shadows.

Reviving my weary heart,
With the longing that consumes me.
The warmth of your affection,
Embedded deeply within my being.

Oh, how I yearn to bloom as a,
Celestial blossom in your fragrant garden.
Spreading love's sweet perfume,
In the sanctuary of your embrace.

Agony of Love

In the luminous dance of night's embrace,
I find solace in the Moon's soft glow,
And in the intoxicating depths of Wine's grace.

Your eyes, like enchanting orbs of magic,
Weave a spell upon my very soul,
Drawing me into the bittersweet agony of love's tragic.

Oh, beloved, you are the essence of beauty refined,
The most exquisite love my heart has ever known,
In your presence, my spirit finds solace, entwined.

You, my angel, ignite the fire in my heart,
With every glance, you stir untold delight,
Forever enslaved by your allure, I am bound to play my part.

As the radiant sun kisses the horizon's edge,
I pledge myself to you, my beloved sunshine,
To cherish you in every whispered pledge.

Yet, amid tears that blur the sight,
I find you dwelling in realms beyond my grasp,
Leaving me to wander in the lonely night.

Once more, I am ensnared by solitude's haunting embrace,
A heart fractured, a silent plea unleashed,
Longing to flee love's relentless chase.

Take your dreams, your wings, and fly,
Why return to flutter within my aching heart?
Release me from this wistful sigh.

Wretched

In twilight's embrace,
In the tempest of time,
In the deluge of fate,
As love's eternal devotee,
I lingered upon an immortal stage,
Yearning for your embrace.

A crown of thorns adorns my brow,
Robes drenched in scarlet hue.

Swept away,
By time's relentless gale,
And destiny's raging torrent.

The vultures lingered
Entangled by the fate's curse,
In the cruel clasp of
destiny's talons.

I lamented in anguish.
As tears welled up,
Tracing the contours of
my solitary heart.
In the tumult of
existence's strife,
I sought redemption,
a solace unrevealed.

Amid the chaos of
Armageddon,
Only my mortal shell and
memories of you endure,
A testament to love's
enduring flame,
Amidst the fleeting
shadows of time.

Cognitive Bliss

Oh my beloved!
Our souls embrace in tranquility.

Take my hands, cold and damp
Long for our minds to blend
Until we are lost in the divine ecstasy
of becoming nothing.

And here we stand,
Upon destiny's brink,
Of a life that we dreamt
before we embrace our fate.

To Heaven's heights or Hell's depth,
We travel forth in love's embrace.

Floral Melody

In the realm of my dreams, heavy
snowflakes descend from the sky.

The purple clouds entice me,
as the rain begins to drizzle.

In the moonlight she unfurls like an
enchanted flower.

A gentle breeze rustle through my being.
As love blossoms,

It metamorphoses me,
Into an enchanted gardener
Of her exquisite garden.

Spirit, Love, Rain

If you are with someone
You long to be alone.

When you are alone
A ghostly essence hover behind you!

Underneath the velvet sky,
Dreams softly sigh.

Heavy clouds loom
And all night it rained!

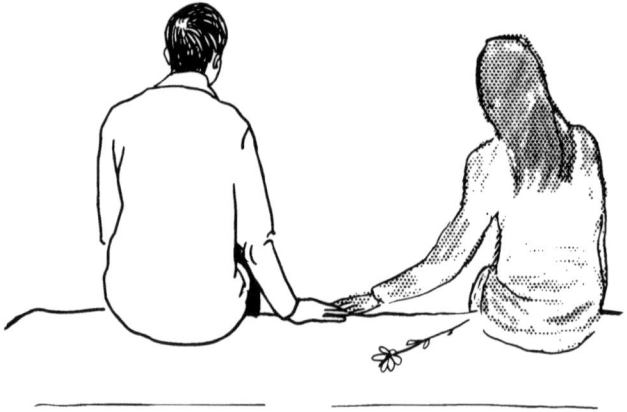

In Exile

Without rain tears,
Without rainbows,
Without Fauna's dance,
Without Flora's delight,
In realms of exile,
Mapped and wide
All souls are but, wanderers, side by side.

In the backyard of my villa,
I dwell, and dance in hues,
A vibrant trance.

I play a life of colorants,
Amid stray cats and doves of gray,
I weave my dreams, day by day.

A Summer Symphony

Upon a summer's breeze,
tranquil, parched, and still.

I wandered down the dusty trail,
where memories distill.

Beside the pathway, etched in
mud, the oxen's journey told.
Each print, a tale of labor,
of stories yet to unfold.

In the embrace of an ancient homestead,
Painted with the hues of memory,
Each moment etched upon its walls,
A cherished treasury.

Savoring every fragment,
Lingering in its embrace,
Yearning for dreams untouched,
Seeking solace in this space.

Here, a gallery unfolds,
Filled with the whims of youth,
Each memory a brushstroke,
Revealing life's truth.

In this picturesque haven,
Where time and tales intertwine,
A symphony of nostalgia,
Where hearts and memories align,
Of bygone sorrows.

The palm trees swayed in warm gusts,
The blabber birds assembled

Their melodies weave tales, rich and free,
Echoing sorrows of days long gone.
Far from the peaks where eagles soar,
Drums' rhythms resonate, men's spirits roar.

In reverence, the stone deity stands,
Embraced by worship's gentle hands.

Into the woods, I seek solace deep,
Where tranquility whispers, secrets to keep.

In holiday's fervor, memories lie,
To await my return beneath the vast sky.

As time dances, awaiting its chance,
I yearn for the Mango rains' sweet trance.

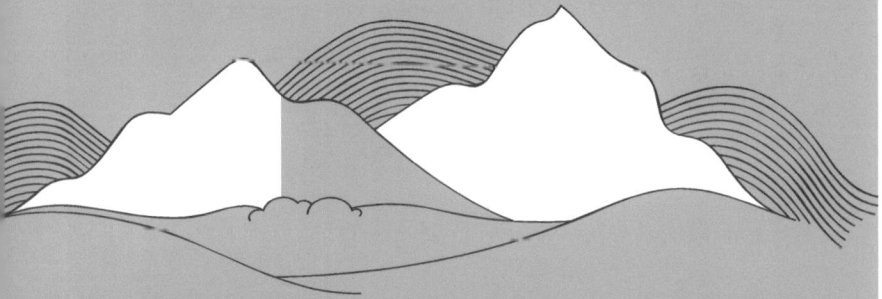

Acknowledgements

A warm expression of gratitude to my
trusted designer Rashmi Kulkarni,
for the wonderful illustrations and book design
infused with creativity.

Thank you
Salim Abdul Rahman,
for the unwavering support and
belief in me.

Furthermore, I wish to express
my heartfelt gratitude to all my friends
notably Siju Ravi, Madhavan Menon and
SreeValsan Mangalassery,
for their unwavering support
in the creation of this book.